VIDEO GAMES

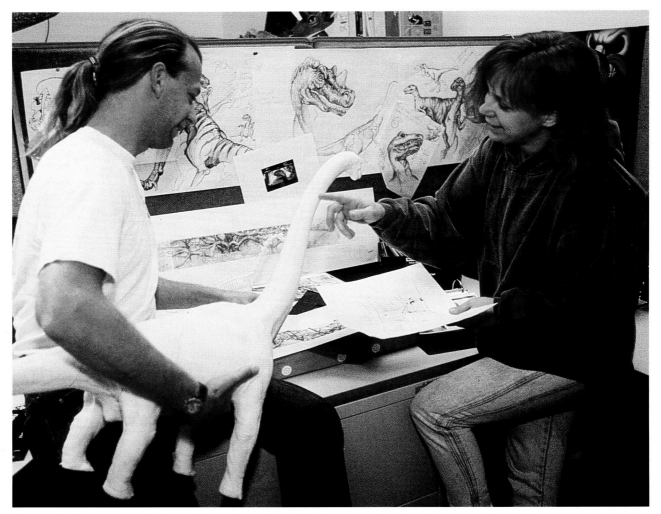

Game designers used three-dimensional models to recreate the dinosaurs from the movie Jurassic Park.

VIDEO GAMES

Arlene Erlbach

Lerner Publications Company • Minneapolis

Dedicated to my husband, Herb, who knows about computers, and to my son, Matthew, who loves to play video games—A. E.

Illustrations by Jackie Urbanovic

Words printed in **bold** are explained in the glossary on pages 43 and 44.

Text copyright © 1995 by Arlene Erlbach
Illustrations copyright © 1995 by Lerner Publications Company

This book is available in two editions:
Library binding by Lerner Publications Company
Soft cover by First Avenue Editions
241 First Avenue North
Minneapolis, MN 55401

ISBN: 0-8225-2389-2 (lib. bdg.)
ISBN: 0-8225-9739-X (pbk.)

Library of Congress Cataloging-in-Publication Data

Erlbach, Arlene.
    Video Games/Arlene Erlbach.
        p. cm.—(How it's made)
    Includes index.
    ISBN 0-8225-2389-2
    1. Video games—Juvenile literature. [1. Video games. 2. Games.]
I. Title. II. Series: Erlbach, Arlene. How it's made.
GV1469.3.E75 1994
794.8—dc20   93-36086

Manufactured in the United States of America
2 3 4 5 6 7 – JR – 01 00 99 98 97 96

CONTENTS

Video games are made in three common formats: the arcade game, the home game that you hook up to your TV, and the handheld game, shown above.

From Pinball to Home Video

Battle alien warriors! Defeat frightening monsters! Be a star at sports! You can do all this and more with video games—and you're the one in control. With video games, you can be involved in exciting situations you'd never encounter in real life.

More than one-third of all American households owns a video game system. Almost 9 billion dollars a year are spent on video games. If all that money were yours, you could buy yourself over 200 million game cassettes. That's enough to play more than 7,000 games a day for 80 years!

The video game craze began in the 1930s with pinball machines. People played pinball in drugstores, restaurants, or arcades. Players pushed a penny or nickel into a slot. They pulled a plunger. Balls knocked over pins. Lights rang and bells flashed. Points added up, encouraging kids to keep playing.

You can still play pinball, but now it's electronic. A computer inside the modern pinball machine provides special effects and adds up points.

Pinball was very popular for decades. Then in the early 1970s, a man named Nolan Bushnell invented a game that was different from anything anyone had seen before. It contained a simple computer that could draw and move objects on a screen. Players pressed buttons to move rectangular "paddles." The paddles hit a ball back and forth across the screen. The game, called Pong, was an electronic version of table tennis. Pong was popular in bars and pizza places. It was the first nationally recognized arcade video game.

Around the same time, inventor Ralph Baer came up with a home video game system named Odyssey. It included a game similar to Pong. Odyssey was an instant success, and video games became common home entertainment.

Pong was a very simple game with a black-and-white screen. But in the early 1970s, it was new and exciting. Because of Pong, coin-operated games replaced pinball machines across the country.

After Odyssey came video games that intro-
duced characters, like Pac-Man, the fuzzy-edged
circle that chomped up rows of dots. But in these
early games, pictures were crudely drawn com-
pared to what you see on your screen now. You'd
probably find the old games boring and wouldn't
want to play them. Video games are more exciting now because they have better sound effects
and **graphics.**

*Two popular characters: Sega's
Sonic Hedgehog, and Mario, from
Nintendo's Super Mario Brothers*

You still can play video games at an arcade. But the most popular video games are home systems you hook up to your TV. These games have four main parts: the game deck, the screen (which is usually your TV set), the controls, and the cassette, called a game pak. The game pak is what you usually refer to when you say "Let's trade," or "I'm going to buy a new game."

A home video game system is a complicated toy, which is actually a computer. To understand how video games are made, you need to understand how they work. So, let's turn the page and see what's inside your deck, controls, and game pak.

The game deck and controls of a home video game system

11

How It Works

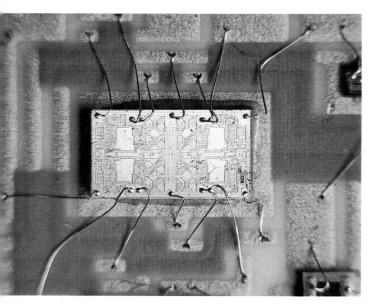

A chip wired to a motherboard

Whether your system is a 16-bit, 32-bit, or 64-bit, it is a kind of computer. A system that contains more **bits,** or units of information, is a more powerful computer. That's why a 32-bit system looks sharper than a 16-bit, has better sound, and has characters that move in more directions.

If you opened a game deck and looked deep inside, you'd see a board with flat metal rectangles attached. The board is called a **motherboard.** Inside the rectangles are **chips,** tiny clay squares about the size of your smallest fingernail. They're made from a special clay called **silicon.**

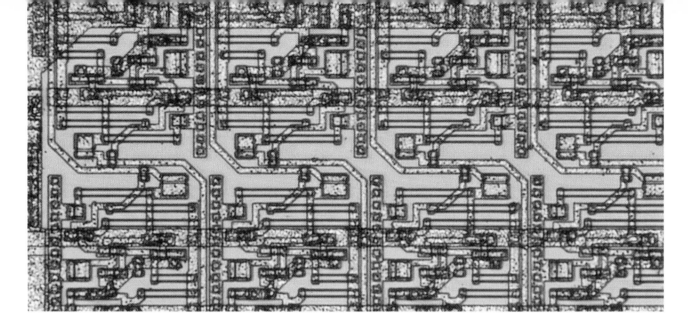

The surface of a chip, enlarged, is a maze of circuits.

If you examined a chip under a microscope, you'd see lots of lines zigzagging across it, like the lines in a maze. These lines are tracks, or **circuits,** that direct electricity where it needs to go when you play your game. Electricity follows these circuits like a train follows tracks.

One of the biggest chips on the motherboard is the **central processing unit,** or CPU. The CPU is the game's brain. The CPU receives game instructions from the game pak, and from you, when you press the controls. It sends these messages to other parts of the deck. It's like a traffic cop, directing every electrical signal.

Another chip on the motherboard is the **picture processing unit,** or PPU. The PPU takes the messages it receives from the CPU and changes them into video signals that will end up as **pixels,** or picture elements. Together, these thousands of dots make up one picture on the screen.

The PPU receives and translates information very fast. The picture on your screen is redrawn 3,600 times per minute, or 60 times per second. Because the pictures change so quickly, the characters look like they're moving. They're not. They're just flashing by your eyes too quickly for your eyes to sort them out.

Your game controls contain an important chip, too. It's called the **shift register.** When you push a button, the shift register sends a message to the CPU. That's how the CPU knows you want your characters to move.

There are other important parts of the game deck. One is the **72-pin connector.** Information travels from the game pak through the connector to the CPU. The connector is like an expressway and the information is like lots of cars, each one carrying messages to the CPU.

Video images (opposite page) *are made up of tiny squares called pixels. These pixels have been enlarged about eight times.*

Another part of the game deck is the **radio frequency (RF) modulator.** It receives video signals from the PPU and helps translate these signals into pictures that appear on your screen, the same way your TV receives signals from a TV station. So, in a way, your deck is like a TV station.

Finally, there is the **random access memory** chip, or RAM, which is like the computer's notepad. It keeps track of your moves and the points you receive.

Now let's look inside the game pak. It has from two to four chips inside. These chips are called **read-only memory** chips, or ROM. In a regular computer, ROM is already installed. But you insert a new, temporary ROM in a video game deck whenever you change game paks. A game deck is really a special kind of computer without any ROM.

The ROM chips inside a game pak have game instructions stored on them in a special code. The instructions tell the CPU what game you are playing, and all the game rules. Your game pak also contains a security chip. This chip keeps you from playing one company's game on another company's deck.

Here's what happens when you play a game:

As soon as you put the game pak into your deck, the information from the ROM chips in your game pak passes through the deck's 72-pin connector. The signals go into the CPU. The CPU sends these messages to the PPU. The PPU converts the messages into video signals and sends the signals to the RF modulator. The RF modulator sends the signals to your TV screen. Then you can start playing your game.

As you push the buttons on the controls, the signals go through the shift register to the CPU.

GAME PAK

GAME DECK

16

The CPU picks up these instructions and sends them to all the chips and other parts of the deck. This makes the characters on the screen move the way you want.

As you play, RAM chips keep track of your score and moves. Everything happens very fast! The system can translate each zap of a character and add up your score in less than a second.

If you're playing a game with a CD-ROM drive, the special game pak doesn't contain ROM like a regular game pak does. All the game information is on the disc instead.

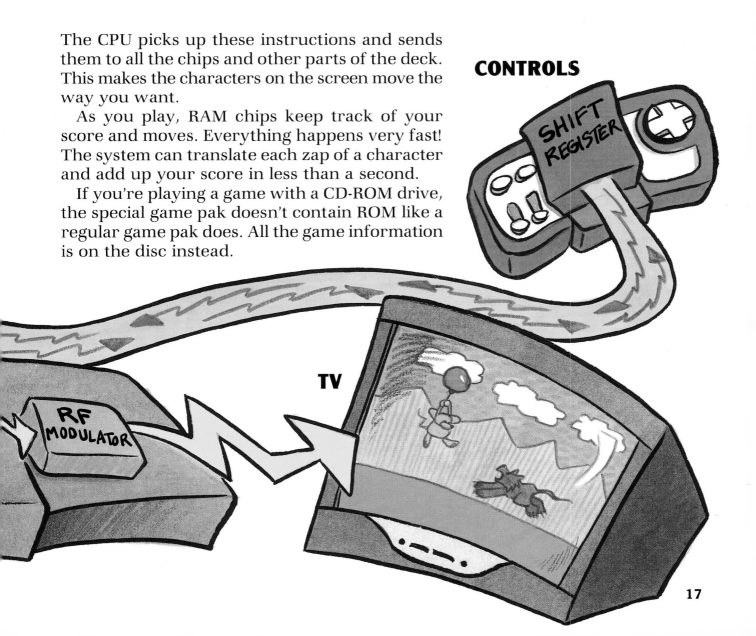

CONTROLS

SHIFT REGISTER

RF MODULATOR

TV

It takes teamwork to design a video game.

3
Game Design

It doesn't matter whether a game is designed for a home video system, a handheld system, or an arcade. Games are all developed in the same way. A group of game experts, called a creative team, designs a video game. The members of the team are the game designer or designers, video artists, sound effects designers, and computer programmer. The team works together for a long time. Creating one video game can take almost a year.

First the creative team decides on the new game's basic style. Will it be a shooting game, a maze game, a racing game, or a game with characters that kick and punch? Next, the team decides what the game will be about. Will it feature detectives, monsters, aliens, stone age characters, or sports figures?

Above: *The Teenage Mutant Ninja Turtles are characters who kick and punch.* Right: *Virtual Racing features speeding cars.*

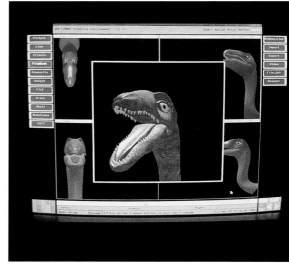

Sometimes, a video game company and a movie studio arrange to have a game and a movie come out at the same time. If the game will be a movie tie-in, the team needs to watch the movie being made and read the script. Then the team selects actions from the movie that would appeal to video game players.

The team makes up a game story. The story must have a beginning, a middle, and an end, just like a movie or a book. The team members decide on a scoring system and rules. Then they talk about the action. As the creative team works, each person takes lots of notes.

If a movie is popular with kids, it is often turned into a video game. Do you remember The Little Mermaid *and* Jurassic Park?

- The armed forces use video simulations of battles to train soldiers.

- Action-adventure and role-playing games are the most popular.

- Space War was the first computer game. The only people who played it were people who worked in the computer industry. It was too difficult for anyone else to play.

If the game is going to be played in an arcade, the action needs to start fast. Arcade players want their money's worth of action right away. If it's a home game, it should have different skill levels, so that players will stay interested in the game for a long time. The same game often comes out in different versions: one for arcades, one for home systems, and a simpler version for handheld systems.

Once the members of the creative team decide on the game style, game story, and the action, they discuss graphics and sound effects. They think about how the graphics will look. Will they be lifelike or cartoonlike—or a combination of the two?

Creating new imaginary worlds is part of a game designer's job.

Pictures and Sound

Video artists take many steps to create the dazzling pictures you see on your game screen. First, they make drawings on **storyboards,** large sheets of paper printed with rows of boxes. The artists sketch inside the boxes, showing the characters in different poses. They draw arrows pointing in the directions the characters will move. The artists usually write notes about the characters on the storyboards, too. They describe the characters' movements and tell what the characters will do.

The artists' first step in creating graphics is to sketch their ideas on paper.

23

Pictures for video games are created in one of two ways. One method is called **converted graphics.** In this method, the artist draws pictures on a computer screen using a control device called a **mouse.** The artist moves the mouse on a flat surface next to the computer. The mouse controls a pointer that draws on the screen.

This artist is drawing pictures with the mouse she holds in her right hand.

Another way of creating graphics for video games is with **digitization.** This is a process that changes hand-drawn pictures or photographs into computer signals. Digitization is often used to create games with lifelike characters. Here's one example of how digitization works:

First, the artist finds real people to model the characters. If the game is a movie tie-in, actors from the movie might be used. In sports games, actual team members might agree to be characters. If the game features lifelike characters who are not movie or sports stars, then the artist chooses models to play the characters. The artist creates costumes and props for the characters. The models dress up for the parts, just like actors do for a movie or play.

Next, one of the models walks or runs on a moving platform called a treadmill, or performs other movements. As the person moves, a video camera tapes the action. The video tape is played on a screen called an **RGB (red-green-blue) monitor,** which is hooked up to a computer. An RGB monitor looks like a TV screen but displays sharper, brighter pictures.

This man is dressed to play a character in a new video game. When he jumps in the air, a video camera captures the action.

The artist views the character moving and decides which **frames,** or individual shots, look best. These are saved on the computer to be used to make the video game. Six to ten frames will have to be put together to show a character walking or running just one step. Four or five frames are needed to show a punch. These frames will flash quickly across your screen, again and again, each time you play the game.

The background of a game might be made with converted graphics or with digitized images of drawings or photographs. Sometimes the background is a combination of the two. What you see on your game screen is often a collage—a collection of many types of separate images.

- People spend over 4 billion dollars a year on video games at arcades. That's 16 billion quarters in all. If you stacked them sideways, they'd reach from the South Pole to past the equator!

- The average arcade player plays about three hours per week.

- Each time someone visits an arcade, he or she spends about three to five dollars.

Creating the background is an important job. The background needs to add to the game's look without overpowering the characters.

Artists recreated a dinosaur's habitat for the background of the Jurassic Park game.

Listen to the voices, grunts, and shouts on your video games. Do they sound real? If they do, they were probably recorded like this.

A video game's sound effects are produced in a sound studio. Sound designers use many of the same recording methods that are used to make records and compact discs.

If a person's voice is needed for a game, someone speaks into a microphone. The voice is recorded onto **digital audio tape,** or DAT. For sound effects like trains, foghorns, or zooming planes, the video company can choose from a library of different sounds that are already on tape. Or, sound tapes can be ordered from other companies with huge sound catalogs. These sound effects are recorded onto DAT, too.

From the tape, all the sounds go through a device called a **synthesizer.** The synthesizer translates the sounds into a code that the computer in your deck can understand. Then all this information is transferred onto a ROM chip that will go inside your video game pak.

A synthesizer is another kind of computer. It can alter sounds and translate them into computer codes.

Programming
the Game

Even though a computer seems smart, it is actually a dumb machine. It can only do what it's told. It doesn't know how and when certain graphics should appear on the screen. It doesn't know when certain sounds should be heard. It needs directions in a detailed set of instructions called a **computer program.** A computer program is written in a special language that's like a code.

There are many different computer programming languages. Game programmers usually use languages called Assembler or C +. These are difficult languages to understand unless you are an experienced computer programmer. But you might know a language called BASIC. It's a computer language that's easy for beginners to learn. You may have learned BASIC at home or at school.

Let's pretend you need to draw a triangle for a computer game. If you have a BASIC program and a computer, you can use this program to draw a triangle and print it on paper. Each separate instruction is a command.

Your triangle will look like the one in the printout pictured below:

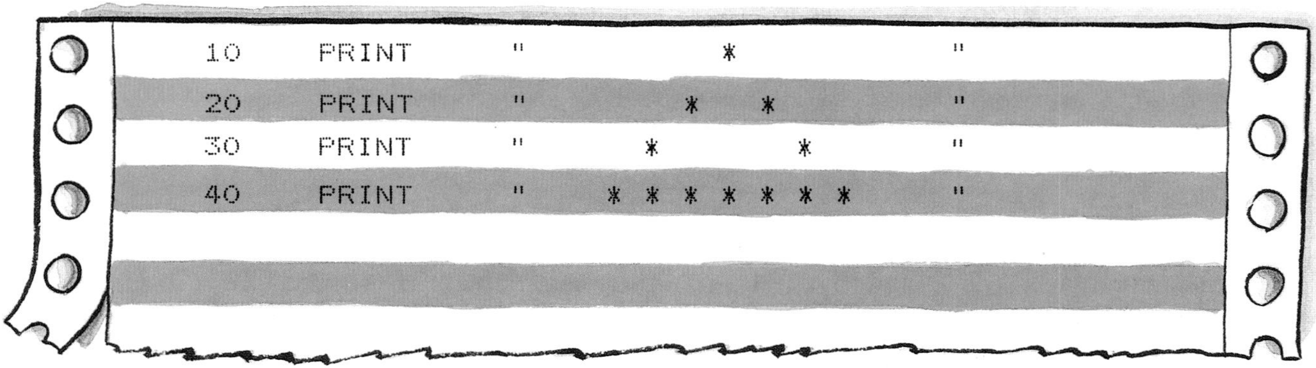

```
10      PRINT       "              *              "
20      PRINT       "           *     *           "
30      PRINT       "        *           *        "
40      PRINT       "     *  *  *  *  *  *  *      "
```

Here's a program that will create a tune:

```
10      Scale$ = "CDEFGAB"
20      PLAY "L16"
30      FOR i% = 0 to 6
40              PLAY "O" + STR$(i%)
50              PLAY "X" + VARPTR$('   le$)
60      NEXT i%
```

It took four commands to draw the triangle, and six to play the tune. But a video game has many more pictures and sounds than this, so the programmer writes lots and lots of commands. The movements of a character's foot might take as many as 100 instructions. So might a character's grunt or growl. An entire game is made up of about 250,000 individual instructions. To print them out, you'd need more than 3,000 sheets of paper!

The programmer writes separate programs for graphics and sounds. Sometimes the programs are stored together on the chips in your game pak. In some games, the graphics and sound programs are on separate chips.

Computer programming takes skill and patience.

It takes a programmer a long time to write a game program—about seven months. As the programmer works on the game, he or she tests it from time to time. The programmer needs to check if the commands make the characters move and sound like the creative team originally intended. If not, the program needs to be changed.

Once the program is completed, all the information is burned onto chips. Then a test team plays the game for a few weeks.

- Kids in the Midwest and northeastern United States spend more time playing video games than do kids in the southern states or on the West Coast.

- On the average, boys play home video games six or seven times each week.

- Girls play home video games about five times per week.

- The first handheld video games hit the market in 1976.

If the game gets the team's approval, several sets of RAM chips are made. Then the chips are sent to a factory where millions of copies are produced. They're assembled into the plastic cases that we call game paks. The game paks are put into protective sleeves, and they're packed into cardboard boxes. Directions are enclosed. Soon, the game paks will be shipped to stores, and a brand-new game will be on the shelf for you to buy or rent.

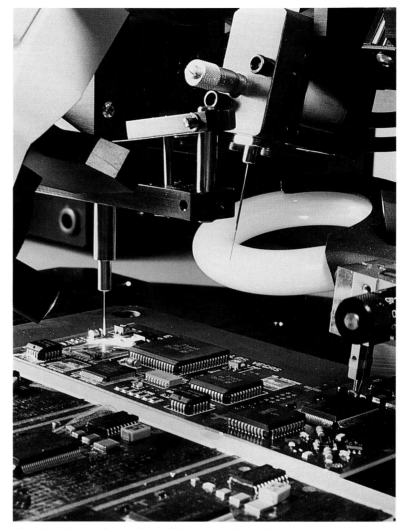

A robotic device wires chips to a board.

Other Kinds of Video Games

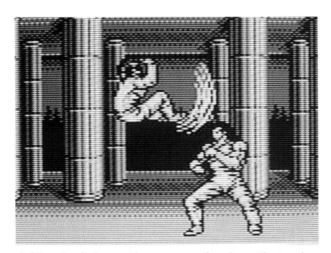

LCDs don't have the range of colors that other games do.

Handheld video games with interchangeable game paks are a lot like miniature home games. But there are a few differences. For one thing, a handheld game has a CPU and PPU that are combined in one chip. And, of course, a handheld game's screen is built into the game. The screen is called a **liquid crystal display,** or LCD. Liquid crystals are sandwiched between two pieces of glass. When you press the buttons on your handheld game, electricity passes through the LCD, creating the images on the screen.

A look inside an arcade game reveals hundreds of chips.

TIME'S UP!

Arcade games offer the best pictures and sound. The computers inside them are very powerful. If you looked inside an arcade game, you'd see hundreds of chips on the game's board. Arcade games sometimes contain one separate computer for sound effects and one for the rest of the game. The computer inside has been programmed so that when you put in your coins, it starts the game. And that's only if you insert the correct coins: The program won't respond to kids' tricks, like putting in the wrong coins or fake tokens.

- Seventy percent of all American kids have a video game system in their homes.

- The average kid will play video games for 212,160 minutes of his or her life. That's a total of 147 days, or 21 weeks!

- Some communities have passed laws limiting the time kids can play video games.

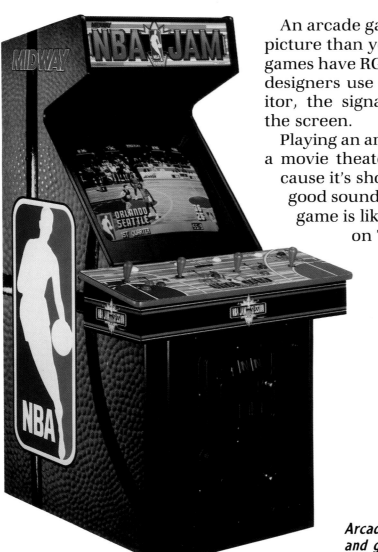

An arcade game's monitor gives you a sharper picture than your TV screen does. Some arcade games have RGB monitors, like the one the game designers use in the studio. With an RGB monitor, the signals go straight from the CPU to the screen.

Playing an arcade game is like seeing a movie at a movie theater. It looks and sounds good because it's shown on a high-quality screen with good sound equipment. Playing a home video game is like renting a movie and watching it on TV. It's fun, and you may want to do it again and again, but you'll miss some of the best razzle-dazzle special effects.

Arcade games offer exciting sound effects and graphics.

How to Win

Every game has special secrets and strategies. Winning tips for the most popular games are being published all the time. Here are some tips that apply to most video games:

1. Always keep a game's directions. Read them over carefully. Sometimes they offer hints about winning.

2. Play the game a lot. Once you learn the basic game, you'll be able to test new strategies.

3. Learn the game story well. This hint applies to sports and maze games as well as role-playing and adventure games. Remember your on-screen enemies, friends, and helpful objects.

4. Press the pause button from time to time and observe the screen. You might figure out things you didn't notice before—techniques that you might use to conquer your opponent. Pausing and observing is especially helpful in role-playing games.

5. Keep your eyes open for characters' special weapons and moves.

6. Remember patterns. If a big yellow wizard comes out after you destroy all the gremlins, you need to zap the wizard fast, every time. Pay careful attention to the challengers in sports games, too. Actions always repeat themselves.

7. Keep notes on what you learn about a game and go over them often.

8. In role-playing and adventure games, be careful about using your ammunition. If you use it all at once, you'll be in a weak position for further attacks.

9. When you enter a new level, room, or land, size up the situation. You'll be ready for what might happen next. This is a good time to use the pause and observe technique.

10. Discuss your game strategies with other players. They may have ideas you hadn't thought of.

11. Read game magazines. They offer tips from experts and avid players.

12. Sometimes the people at rental stores can offer suggestions.

8

Choosing a Home Video Game

Games are expensive, so it's important to choose one you'll play with for a while. Here are tips for making wise choices:

1. What sound effects are in the game? Will you want to listen to them for hours and hours?

2. Are the graphics interesting enough to keep you playing the game over and over again?

3. What's the warranty on the game? Who is responsible for repairs—you or the manufacturer?

4. Are the directions clear and easy to understand?

5. Is the game challenging, yet not too hard? Nobody wants a game that's impossible to win.

6. Can your system run the game as it is? Or do you need to buy more equipment?

7. Friends are a good source of information. Try a game at a friend's house a few times before you buy it yourself.

8. Renting games is a good way to try a game, too.

9. Game magazines often rate games. Usually, they rate games separately on graphics, sound effects, and level of challenge. These ratings give players a chance to choose a game based on the factors that are most important to them.

10. Most of all—is this game fun? And is it one you'll want to play again and again?

MONEY-SAVING TIP

Have a swap meet with your friends. Everyone can bring their old games and trade. Some towns even hold organized swap meets. After participants pay a few dollars for admission, they can try out games, trade them, and discuss winning tips. Swap meets are usually announced in the Friday or weekend edition of the entertainment section of your local paper. You can start your own swap meet at your school, church, synagogue, or community center. You could offer to donate the money you collect for admission.

Video Game Care

1. Keep your games' warranties in a safe place. A warranty entitles you to free repairs if you need them within a specific time. The warranty is written on a card or slip of paper and packed in the box with your video game.

2. Store each game in its sleeve and box to protect it from dust.

3. Make sure your deck is free of dust, too. Dust in the 72-pin connector can block signals so that your deck won't work.

4. Turn off the deck when you're not using it.

5. Remove game paks from the deck whenever you aren't using them.

6. Keep game paks off the floor, so that nobody steps on them.

7. Lend or borrow just one game at a time. It's easy to forget who has what if you're involved in too many lend-outs.

8. Don't eat or drink while you play your games. Crumbs and spills ruin games.

9. Store all your game paks in a special place when you aren't using them.

10. If you think you need a repair, go to a VCR and TV repair shop, or a video store. Sometimes you can make a problem worse if you try to fix it yourself.

GLOSSARY

bit: the smallest unit of computer information

central processing unit (CPU): a computer's "brain." The CPU chip receives instructions and sends messages to other chips.

chip: a tiny piece of silicon with electronic circuits on its surface

circuit: a path that directs and carries electricity from place to place

computer program: a series of detailed instructions to be performed by a computer

converted graphics: a method of drawing computer graphics directly on a screen with a mouse

digital audio tape (DAT): magnetic tape on which sound is recorded and played back digitally (with computer signals)

digitization: a process that converts pictures or sounds into computer signals that can be stored on a disc or tape

frame: an individual picture on a length of video tape or film

graphics: visual images (pictures) that are created by a computer

liquid crystal display (LCD): a type of display that uses liquid crystals and an electrical charge to create graphics on a screen. LCDs are often used with handheld video games.

motherboard: the board that contains a computer's main parts. In a game deck, the motherboard contains the CPU, PPU, and RAM.

mouse: a small control device. By moving a mouse on a flat surface, such as a desk, the user can draw images on a computer screen.

picture processing unit (PPU): the part of the game deck that receives messages from the CPU and changes them into video signals

pixels: tiny dots or squares that together make up a complete picture, as on a TV screen

radio frequency (RF) modulator: the part of a game deck that receives video signals from the PPU and translates the signals into pictures

random access memory (RAM): the part of a computer's memory that allows information to be stored temporarily. Because RAM is only temporary, any information left in RAM is lost when the computer is turned off. In video games, RAM chips keep track of your moves and points.

read-only memory (ROM): the part of computer's memory that permanently stores information. A game pak's ROM chips store the instructions for the particular game.

RGB (red-green-blue) monitor: a color monitor that displays especially sharp, clean images. RGB monitors are often used for viewing video tape or in arcade games.

72-pin connector: the part of a video game deck that allows information to pass from the game pak to the CPU

shift register: a chip in the game controls that sends signals from the controls to the CPU

silicon: a type of clay. Silicon is used to make electronic devices because electricity flows through it easily.

storyboard: a large sheet of paper printed with rows of boxes. Video artists use storyboards to sketch characters and scenes.

synthesizer: a computerized device that produces sounds and translates them into computer codes

INDEX

ACKNOWLEDGMENTS

This book would not have been possible without the generous help of the following people and organizations:

Mr. Roger Sharpe, Mr. Jack Haeger, Mr. Jim Greene, Mr. Art Tianis, and Mr. Scott Slomiany of Williams Electronic Games, Inc.; Midway Manufacturing Company, Manufacturers of Bally and Midway Amusement Games; Ms. Jody Privette and Mr. Daniel Kitchen of Absolute Entertainment, Inc.; Ms. Allyne Mills of Acclaim Entertainment, Inc.; Mr. Richard Laurent; and Ms. Cynthia King.

The photographs in this book are reproduced through the courtesy of:

pp. 2, 10 (left), 18, 19 (bottom), 20 (right), 22, 24, 26, 27, Sega of America, Inc.; pp. 8, 37, Williams Electronic Games, Inc.; p. 9, Atari Games Corporation; pp. 10 (right), Nintendo of America, Inc.; pp. 6, 11, Turbo Technologies, Inc.; pp. 12, 13, 34, © Bruce Iverson; pp. 14, 25 (both), 28, 29, 36, Williams Electronic Games, Inc./Art Tianis; pp. 19, 35, Konami, Inc.; p. 20 (left), CAPCOM® USA, Inc.; p. 23, Spectrum Holobyte, Inc.; p. 33, Origin Systems, Inc.; p. 47, Karen Sirvaitis/IPS.

Front and back cover photos courtesy of Sega of America, Inc.

ABOUT THE AUTHOR

Arlene Erlbach has written more than a dozen books of fiction and nonfiction for young people. In addition to being an author, she is an elementary school teacher. She loves to encourage children to read and write, and she is in charge of her school's Young Authors' program. Ms. Erlbach lives in Morton Grove, Illinois, with her husband, her son, a collie, and three cats.